IF ONLY THE WALLS COULD HEAR

Teresa Sewell

Copyright © 2021 by Teresa Sewell

All rights reserved. This book or any portion thereof may not be reproduced or used in any manner whatsoever without the express written permission of the publisher except for the use of brief quotations in a book review.

Printed in the United States of America

First Printing, 2021

ISBN: 978-0-578-34872-8

Email: sewellteresa0@gmail.com

DEDICATION

To my daughters, you are my angels. The first time I saw you both I knew God had blessed and entrusted me to be the mom of two beautiful daughters that have grown to be amazing phenomenal black women. They are blessings from God. I love you so much!

To my parents, I love you so much you are the reason I have become the woman I am today. Thank you for your prayers, great support, and continuous care.

ACKNOWLEDGMENT

My completion of this project could not have been accomplished without my mom Murrilene Sewell for pushing and reminding me to start and get it done! Thank you for your care, love, prayers, and encouragement through this process. I truly thank God for you! God could not have blessed me with a better mom!

To my daughters Jessica and Keli Pitts who encourage me to continue to grow and never never give up on my dreams I am so grateful for your love and support. I love you!

To my spiritual mom, Ms. Gladys Flournoy, thank you for your continuous prayers, love, care, and support. Continue to be on fire for God! I love you!

To everyone who has been a part of my life and I cannot express enough thanks for continued love, support, and prayers for me along the way I would never forget you! I love each and every one of you!.

Table of Contents

Introduction 1

Chapter 1: A Blessed Family 3

Chapter 2: If They Only Knew 6

Chapter 3: I Couldn't Believe My Eyes 9

Chapter 4: Time For A Change 12

Chapter 5: Not Ms, Perfect 15

Chapter 6: My Answer Is Yes 18

Chapter 7: Its Time 20

Chapter 8: Surprise Again 22

Chapter 9: A Belly Full 23

Chapter 10: The Honeymoon Is Over 25

Chapter 11: Dejavu 26

Chapter 12: Finding Myself 29

Chapter 13: Yes Again 32

Chapter 14: The Rejection 36

Chapter 15: A New Change 38

Chapter 16: What Happened To Daddy's Little Girls? 40

Chapter 17: No Means No. 43

Chapter 18: The Blame Game 45

Chapter 19: Oh, Honey, I Am Done!!! 47

INTRODUCTION

Today is Wednesday, October 26th, 2016, at 8:36A.M

It is such a beautiful morning, and things are looking much brighter today. I feel the presence of the Lord with me. I am feeling the Spirit of praise coming upon me. I don't know what will happen, but I feel like the doors of confusion, anxiety, doubt, and low self-esteem are closing in my life that are still open. As I sit here and write, I feel the Spirit of peace rushing through my body.

I'm beginning to heal from the pain of life that has wrapped itself inside of me. The burden that I was carrying is beginning to lift out of me, and off of me, I no longer carry that weight. Oh, what a sense of joy I am feeling!

I hear the Lord saying everything is okay, trust, and believe in Him.

I sit here and reminisce over my life and see how God has kept me.

I can't say anything but thank you, Jesus! There were many days that I questioned myself and God asking Him why? Why was it necessary for me to go through what I did? Then I ask, what have I done to deserve His precious love, protection, and peace of mind? I realize it's no goodness of my own, but it is the Lord Jesus Christ.

Now I understand why I had to go through what I went through. I can now share my testimony with you as you read my story. I pray for every man and woman who has to go through heartache, abuse, and misuse, whether verbal or physical.

God can and will bring you healed, whole, and forgiven when you surrender all to Him.

That's why I can share my testimony with you now.

Come and go with me on my life journey.

CHAPTER 1

A BLESSED FAMILY

My name is Teresa; it all began in the 1970s in Atlanta. I was a timid little girl. I grew up in a family with a father and mother in a household. I had great parents. My dad was an excellent provider. He was a hard-working father who took great care of his family. He made sure that every need was met, and he spent a lot of time with them. Every Friday night, the family went to the wrestling shows, and every Saturday night, we would go to the movies. I loved my family.

My mom was the best. She did a great job as a wife and mom. My mom made sure that the meals were prepared on time every day; we were clean dressed nicely, and she did other things that needed to be done in the home.

My parents gave me and my siblings everything that we asked for.

I wanted to do a lot of things, and I did. I was a member of the Girls Club; I took swimming lessons, gymnastic, cheerleading, just to name a few. We were a happy family with a happy life together.

One day, at the age of 5, my mom made sure that I was dressed and looking nice like she always does so I could go outside and play. While walking out the door, a small child who lived above me dropped a brick on my head. The little boy ran away, and I screamed to the top of my lungs, and my mom ran out the door, and I was standing there with blood running down my face crying. My mom panicked. She finally calmed down, took me in the house, put a towel on my head, got my sisters together, and took me to the Children's Hospital. The nurses rushed me to the back, and there they put stitches in my head.

When my parents found out why the little boy dropped the brick on my head, they were furious. He said he wanted to touch my private area.

As a 5-year-old little girl, you are not thinking about little boys, especially when you are told not to let them touch your private parts.

The following week was Halloween, and I went out the door to play. I was hit in the eye with an egg, so I had to go back to the hospital. This time I didn't have to get stitches. Now at this point, my parents were fed up and decided it was time to move. They found a new house for us. My sisters and I were pretty delighted to be in our very first house. Some weeks later, my family and I moved to our new home. We were very excited. We now had a fenced-in backyard where we could play. Our parents bought us new bikes, a swing set, and a new dog. It was so beautiful we named him Lassie. He was brown and white and very playful; we had fun playing at our new house.

I remember it was our first Christmas in our new home. This was the best time for us.

On Christmas Eve, my dad and I would go to this little store called Hardees in the West End to get some fruit and candy for Christmas, and he would tell me we had to get back before Santa Clause came. He can't see me up, or I would not get anything on my list. I would be excited to go to bed that night.

The following day was Christmas; my sisters and I would get up and run to the living room and find a lot of toys on our list and more. There would be a beautiful fruit and candy basket that my mom had made for us on the table. I can tell she put a lot of love into making these boxes for us.

If Only The Walls Could Hear

They had a lot of candy and fruit in them. We would go to their room and wake them up and ask them to come into the living room with us. My parents would ask what Santa Claus brought us? We would say come and see with so much excitement. I wrote Santa a letter that night while my sisters were asleep to thank him for bringing my sisters and me the things on our list and the happiness and joy he brought to our house on Christmas.

One particular Christmas, I called my cousin, who I was very close to ask her what she got for Christmas. I felt sad because she didn't get what she wanted. I knew her mom was a single mom with 8 children. My aunt tried to do her best to provide for her family. I asked my aunt and my parents if my cousin could come over to my house on Christmas, and they said yes. My parents said they would buy her something and she stayed with us that whole week. Seeing that smile on my cousin's face when she got the doll and clothes she wanted to be made me so happy.

I realized at that moment that my sisters and I were blessed.

CHAPTER 2

IF THEY ONLY KNEW

Something begins to happen in our household. It started to change, and we started to see behaviors that children shouldn't see nor hear from their parents as a child. My parents began to have a lot of arguments. One night I overheard my parents fussing about our neighbor who lived behind us. It was a man. My dad thought my mom was having an affair with our neighbor. As time went on, it began to get worse. It started to move from verbal abuse to physical abuse. My dad started to abuse my mom more and more. I could see the hurt and pain in my mom's face when she had to face us. I asked myself how my dad could hit my mom and excuse her for cheating with the neighbor behind us, but my mom would always say she had not done anything. My sisters and I would see the man washing his car when we played in the backyard. He seems like a nice man. I never saw any signs to support my dads' accusations. I never understood why the man who was supposed to be my hero could do such a thing to his wife and our mother.

As a child seeing abuse in my household, never knowing when my dad would hit my mom, it calls fear, anxiety, frustration, and anger. It made me see my dad as another person. I could not believe the man who was a good provider and did many things with my siblings, and I could be that monster to my mom. One day she came home from work, and when she entered the house, my dad hit her with such rage. To see the tears run down my mom's face and the look in my dad's eyes that I couldn't recognize. My siblings and I screamed and told my dad to leave our mother alone.

He was doing all that because he thought she was cheating.

I realized that jealousy, abuse, anger had entered our home.

As a child, you wonder how a man can hit a woman he is supposed to love, especially in front of his kids. That often played in my mind. I asked myself, is that love? Is that something that I have to look forward to one day happening to me.? Is this how a man shows his devotion to his wife? So many questions flooded my mind.

Being a child, it was said that what goes on in the house stays in your house. It's a way of hiding or not confronting the issues at hand. After all, you are ashamed because you don't want the world to see that your life isn't that perfect picture; they would see behind the material things.

People would always say to me that you are spoiled and always get what you want; however, it is not what it looks like.

Imagine a man supposed to be the hero to his family was the enemy to his wife. When you look at my family, everything on the outside looks perfect. We lived in a nice middle-class neighborhood and kept new cars. We acted like we were a delighted, close family; we went out as a family every Friday night when my dad got off from work for the weekend. My cousin always wanted to come over to my house because my parents always bought us things and took us places every week. If they only knew what was going on when they were not there. God, please help my family.

Now while going through this abuse, my mom got pregnant. When I heard the news, I became angry. Something inside of me couldn't be happy for my parents. I started to take my anger out on my sisters and my cousins. When my mom told us she was pregnant, I pushed my sister on the heater in the bathroom, and she burnt her lower arm. My parents punished me and never asked what was wrong. Later that week, I spent the night with my cousins, who bit one of them. Again, I got punished, and they never tried to figure out what was wrong with me. My anger began to worsen, and I didn't know how to control it. Now, mom goes into the hospital to have the baby, delivering a little boy. My aunt, my mom's sister, stayed with us while my mom was in the hospital. She told us the news, and I hit my sister in her left eye with a toy truck and blackened her eye. I got angry because my mom had another baby while our household wasn't in a healthy place to bring a bundle of joy. Especially when joy doesn't live here anymore.

CHAPTER 3

I COULDN'T BELIEVE MY EYES

After my brother turned 10 years old, my mom told my siblings and me that she was going back to work and that her sister would watch us while she went to work. I asked my mom and dad if I could go over to my aunt's house to spend time with my cousin, who was like my sister, and they said yes. I knew it was a way to get some space. I was going over there every week for some days while my mom and dad worked. As I spent a lot of time at my aunt's house, I met other children. One day I met this girl that lived directly across from my aunt. We were suitable for a moment, and then she started maltreating me because some of the boys she was interested in like me, and I didn't live there. I didn't even know the boys she was talking about to me. One week I went to my aunt's house, and my cousin asked me to go to the Big Field with her. They had a summer program where they served box lunches, and the kids could play on the playground. On this particular day, this handsome boy walked up on the playground. He had some beautiful light brown eyes and pretty black curly hair. He walked up to me and asked me if I lived over there? I stared at him, and he had to get my attention. Coming out of a daze, my response was no". I told him I was visiting my cousin, who I pointed to. The girl found out that the handsome boy was talking to me. She came up to the Big Field to pick a fight with me about a boy I didn't know she liked. At that time, the boy had already left.

Teresa Sewell

I was playing on the merry-go-round, and she got on there

This girl was so angry that she pulled my hair, and I fell off the merry-go-round, but my hair got caught, and I was dragged around and around yelling," for help, my cousin came to my rescue. She helped me up as tears rolled down my cheeks. I cried while running back to my aunt's house. She asked me what was wrong, and I told her. She told my cousin and me to come on. We went over to the girl's house to ask for her mom. Her big sister came to the door and said her mom wasn't there. The girl came out the door to say something to me, and my aunt told her to go back in the house, and she continued to come at me. She hit me when I said something back, and my aunt told me that I better defend myself or she was going to continue to mess with me. So I fought back, and I no longer had this issue with her again. I began to release my anger, and I began to change. The bad behavior stopped. I felt so much confidence in myself. The boy continued to come up to the Big Field, and one day I saw him up there, and he asked me for my phone number. He also asked me to be his girlfriend, and I said yes. I am 13 yrs. Old, but my parents still wouldn't let me talk to boys on the phone. So, I talked to him when I saw him at my aunt's house. He would meet me on the Big Field. On Friday, I was excited to meet him on the Big Field, and we walked around talking and laughing; we decided to sit on the wall while still talking, a little boy's ball rolled into the street. My boyfriend went across the street to get the ball and was hit by an 18-wheeler truck in front of me. I screamed so loud I couldn't believe what I had just seen. I ran back to my aunt's house crying and nervous, I asked her if I could go home, and she asked me what was wrong? I couldn't tell her I was in shock. She found out what had happened and she called my mom's sister to pick me up and I went home. Later on, when my mom came home from work, she noticed I was crying and asked me what was wrong. I told her I saw a boy get hit by an 18-wheeler truck. I was crying so hard; my mom hugged me. Weeks later, I couldn't go on the Big Field again or on that street without seeing him lying on the ground. It was becoming hard for me to sleep at night. It took a while for me to sleep without a light on. I missed him so much I could not tell anyone he was my boyfriend, but I had to keep the relationship we had balled inside of me. It felt like we had known each other for years; we were old friends. If only the walls could hear the tears from my eyes that night.

My mind was so full, and my heart was broken.

CHAPTER 4

TIME FOR A CHANGE

Now I'm 14 years old. My parents decided that we needed a bigger house, so it was time to move. We were getting older, and we needed more space. We were excited. I was glad I needed a change. We are now moving from the middle class to an upscale neighborhood with better schools, and I will now have my own room. I thought this was a brand-new start for our family.

I was wrong. The arguments and abuse continued. We had moved away from the man with whom my father had accused my mother of cheating, but at this time, I began to see it for what it was. My dad just liked beating on my mom, and she let him.

I wondered why my mom continued to put up with that abuse. If she was late coming from work, my dad would begin to act out again. It had become routine in the house with us. We acted like we did not see it or hear it. As the years went by, my dad began to change for the better. I don't know what happened, but I believe God was answering my prayers. My dad became this friendly, loving, funny, and caring guy who will give you the shirt off his back; he tells us he loves us and is very affectionate toward my mom and us again.

Thank God for answering my Prayers"!

I started at a new school, and on the first day, I met a girl who lived two streets away. We begin to hang together every day. We ended up being best friends. When we attended school, we hung out together

People would come up to her talking and laughing, but they wouldn't say anything to me, making me feel invisible. I wondered why people wouldn't acknowledge me.

This was happening to me throughout the school with inter issues and all the other stuff I had been going through. I began to feel like I had to make people notice me. I started to attract guys at other schools, but they didn't take me seriously. At 16, my older brother moved in with us, and I started hanging out with him. I later met one of his friends. We started hanging out and getting serious. He took me to my 1st high School prom. That night was amazing. He treated me with such love, respect. He gave me the attention that I needed. Right then, I felt like he was a good guy. We were becoming very close.

As time went on, he told me he had to leave because he was joining the AirForce, and he wanted me to go with him. He asked me to be his wife. I told him I couldn't do that because I was only 17 and wasn't leaving my family. I remember that day he left; my heart was filled with sadness. At that moment, I realized I had just lost the only guy that I felt showed me, love. This was something that I had never imagined I would feel at such a young age. I missed him so much.

I graduated from high school at 17 years old. I started working at Kroger's in the day and with my dad at night on his second job because my parents had bought me a car, but I had to pay the insurance and gas. One night when my dad and I were working, the security guard started a conversation with my dad and me. He asked my dad about the other job he worked at because my dad had a uniform, and he told him he worked for the City of Atlanta.

He asked my dad if the company was hiring. My dad said yes and that he could help him get a job there because he was the supervisor. So, they exchange phone numbers. The security guard called our house, but he asked for me instead. We began to talk and build a relationship. We would talk on the phone for hours, and then we started going out on dates. One night after one of the dates, we stayed in the car until the morning. Wow, talking about our lives and parents. I told the security guard that I was a daddy's girl, which caused a lot of confusion between my mom and me because my dad would give me whatever I would ask him for.

I told him that I was thinking about moving out of my parent's house and moving in with my cousin, but I wanted to find just that one good job that could take care of everything.

So as time moved on, I did find that one good job, and I moved out of my parent's house at 18 years old. I was on my own, and my cousin and I were good roommates.

My boyfriend, the security guard, came over every day; one night, things went a little further than I wanted them to go; that was my first time being intimate with a guy. Everything's happening so fast I need to move back home and refocus on my life. I just started a new job that I like working for the United postal service; I was very excited about this job. Then this happened.

Chapter 5

NOT MS, PERFECT

One morning I woke up feeling sick. I vomited to the point my eyes would turn red, and I would be late for work. My mom started to notice that every morning around 10 am I would start to get sick. She usually took me to the train station, but she would have to wait until I was finished vomiting.

One morning I was getting ready for work, and my mom asked me if I was pregnant. I didn't know how to respond." She said, "I'm going to take you to the doctor." So, you know the results came back positive? Yes, I was pregnant. To look at the disappointment in my mom's eyes crushed me. I didn't know what to say because I felt numb, scared, ashamed. I felt like I had disappointed my parents. I was supposed to be the good one. I was called Ms. Perfect.

There was a lot of silence between my mom and me on the way home. In my mind, I just couldn't believe this was happening and how I was going to tell my boyfriend and my dad. I was terrified. Later that day, my heart started to beat so fast from anxiety because it was time for my dad to come home, and I didn't know what he would say. I tried to stay in my room, so I didn't have to face him and my siblings because I knew my mom had told everyone. So, my dad came home, and he called me to come to him, and my heart-felt like it was going to jump out of my chest. My dad asked me if I had told my boyfriend yet, and" I said no." I didn't know how to tell him. My dad told me I needed to call him and let him know. I was so scared. I didn't know what he would say and how we would take care of a baby. My boyfriend lived with this man he called his dad at that time.

I called my boyfriend, and I was crying, and he asked me what was wrong, and it couldn't come out of my mouth. I finally calmed down, and I told him that I was expecting, and he asked whether I went to the doctor, "I said yes' " I was blown away with his response. He asked me how far along I was, and I said 7weeks. He asked me if I was okay. I said yes, now I am.

Immediately I felt like 100 pounds was lifted off of me.

At this time, he was attending college, and he got a job working there after school. That lasted until summer vacation. He found another job working at a summer camp up the street from his house. He was a summer counselor and lifeguard. He made enough money where he saved so when our baby came, we would be prepared. I left my job because the doctor told me I couldn't work during my pregnancy. I stayed so sick the doctor had to put me on bed rest.

My boyfriend was being so friendly and supportive; he was just fantastic! He would let me drive his car, and he took the bus. The days he drove, he would pick me up; after he got off work and made sure I ate. He bought me clothes that I needed and the food I needed at home. He was an excellent provider. I just knew he would be a great dad and husband one day.

My boyfriend didn't go to work this particular day because he wanted to take me to my ultrasound appointment. I was so excited that I could see our baby for the first time. On the way to the appointment, we discussed what we thought the gender was. He said he wanted a boy, and I wanted a girl. We decided that we didn't want to know. When we left the appointment, he was quiet in the car. I asked him what was wrong, and he said nothing. I didn't feel good about his answer, and my mind wandered. We stopped to eat lunch, and suddenly, he asked me to spend the weekend with him. I told him that I would not spend the weekend at this house because his dad lived there, so he told me that he would get a hotel room for the weekend. So, I said, okay. On the way back home, I kept thinking about what I would say to my parents to explain my weekend absence. I told them that my boyfriend wanted me to go out of town to his grandmother's house. Now, this was around Christmas time. My parents told me to have a good time, and they would like me to be back with the family for the holidays.

Chapter 6

MY ANSWER IS YES

My boyfriend and I left and went to the hotel close to his house. The weekend started great. We were having a good time. We enjoyed each other and got more into each other mentally and physically, and shared our likes, dislikes, hopes, and dreams. Later on, that night, before getting ready for bed, I noticed that my boyfriend started to act weird. He went to the car and returned; he told me to close my eyes with excitement. I stood there anxiously, wanting to know what he was doing. He grabbed my left hand and told me to open my eyes. When I opened my eyes to my surprise, he had some sparkling grape juice, roses, and 2 glasses. He got on his knees and asked me to marry him. I couldn't believe this was real. The ring was beautiful! He said this ring is just temporary. I said yes, yes!!!! I will marry you. We kissed passionately, and he said I'm going to take real good care of you and our baby. The following day was Christmas day, and we packed up to go home. This weekend felt like it wasn't long enough. I left home as a girlfriend, and now I'm a fiance.

I was so excited! so we decided to tell my family the news when we got there. I was surprised everyone was happy except my mom. Later that night, my fiance left, my mom called me in the living room, and she asked me not to marry him. She said he isn't good for you. Trust me! I didn't understand what she meant. My mom said something about him just didn't feel right to her.

I told her he was a good man and would marry him because I loved him.

My mom said to me; I wish you wouldn't marry him. I was thinking how she knew he was not good for me. She never spent time with him.

The following weekend my fiance and I went to tell his aunt and uncle about the marriage, and they were excited. His aunt asked if she could plan the wedding. My fiance wanted to give me the wedding that I wanted. His aunt was good at planning and decorating. I told her she could plan the wedding. She asked me the colors and the things I thought I would like. This took a lot off of me being pregnant. She was very creative. She planned the wedding on a budget.

CHAPTER 7

ITS TIME

So in July 1988, my best friend was down at my house. We went outside to play ball so that I could get some exercise. While playing ball, I started to have pains in my stomach. The pain was coming so fast; it felt unbearable. She went to the door to get my mom. They took me to the hospital, where I was admitted immediately. My best friend called my fiance, and he rushed down to the hospital. When he got there, I was in labor. The doctors said it was too early because my first baby isn't due until September. The doctor said that our baby's lungs aren't developed yet because of the due date beginning in September. Therefore, the doctor stopped the labor pains. A couple of days later, the doctors took some tests because I kept trying to go into labor, and they kept stopping it.

The test came back saying that our baby had a bowel movement and they had to put me in labor. My fiance and I were so scared because we knew our baby would be premature. The doctor came in and put me in labor. I started to feel the pain all over again. This was something that I had never felt before. My heart was beating so fast. I heard other girls screaming on the same floor I had their baby. The contractions were coming faster and faster, and the pain was unbearable. My fiance was great the whole time. Finally, our baby was born. It was a girl; she was adorable! She was 4 pounds and 15 ounces. I saw his face light up! He was so happy! I just cried when they put her in my arms. That's a love you couldn't describe. Our first daughter and I had to stay at the hospital until she gained some weight. I was so excited she gained the weight she needed to go home. We finally came home, and my family spoiled her. My fiance was driving to my parent's house every day to see us. He finally asked me if we could move together. He wanted us to be close to him. My first daughter was born, and we were overjoyed. He was a very loving father to her.

We found an apartment and moved in together, and his father moved in with us. I started to feel like a wife already. I had to take care of our daughter, do laundry, cook, and do other things in our home that had to be done. Now life seems to be getting real. I was 18 years old, engaged, and about to become a mom and take on an enormous home responsibility. My life seemed to be moving too fast. I started to feel depressed and wondered if I had made the right decision to move with my fiance

CHAPTER 8

SURPRISE AGAIN

Months later, I found out that I was pregnant again. Still not married and about to become a mom for the second time. I felt so overwhelmed that I didn't want to keep my baby. My fiance brought me to my senses. My fiance wanted to keep our baby. Here I am, beginning to get sick again. Our 1st daughter is not even 1 year old yet. My fiance's dad took me to my doctor's appointments when my fiance had to work. This made it a little challenging to take care of our 1st daughter, be pregnant again, and be on bed rest. Our 1st daughter was so spoiled that she cried all the time. My future father-in-law helped me with her along with my sisters. No one had told my mom about my second pregnancy.

I moved back in with my parents because his dad was still with us even though he helped me. It was not enough room for all of us, and besides, I needed more help, and I know my family would love to help my babies and me.

My mom is still telling me I shouldn't marry him because something about him wasn't right. I immediately told my mom that I was pregnant again; she was not surprised she said she already knew. My family was a big help to my daughter and me. She was so spoiled. My fiance made it known that he wanted us with him, so he found a place for us. He said we would get married soon. The way he said it was like saying one day but not today.

CHAPTER 9

A BELLY FULL

Now it is time for the wedding on June 24th, 1989. I was 4 months pregnant. This day was supposed to feel exciting; however, I was already in the position of a wife. My fiance's aunt did a fantastic job at the wedding. When I arrived at the church, my friends and cousins at the wedding were already there to help me get ready. This was fun. The people start to come. However, my fiance hasn't arrived yet. He finally showed up 20 min late. A part of me was scared, and another part of me wondered if I was doing the right thing. I felt as if my inner self warned me not to do it, and his delay was a sign. I felt I should continue what I had started, and I didn't want to disappoint anyone. I can still hear my mom say, don't marry him, Teresa.

We lined up at the church, and I grabbed my dad's arm. I felt my fears melting away. Something came over that made me feel like everything would be okay. As I walked down the aisle, as I looked around, I saw all the people that were there and the beautiful pink and white decorations; it brought me to tears. I felt like I was in a wonderland experiencing a fairy tale wedding. My heart started to pound as my dad let my arm go, and I became very hot like an oven lit up inside me. I felt like I was going to pass out. I looked to the right, and I saw my daughter. She was gorgeous, and it made me smile. At that moment, I felt like my daughter and my unborn child were worth everything I was doing. I looked into my fiancee's eyes as we said our vows. He had this look of fear and nervousness on his face. Now it was time to kiss the bride, and I felt a sense of relief that it was over. Wow, now I am officially married. He and I walked down the aisle with joy and happiness. We had the reception at my husband's aunt's house. She had it set up nicely. As we entered the house, there were Pink, White, and Gold flowers everywhere. The food on the table was colorful and looked delicious. All our family and friends came out to celebrate with us. We had a lot of fun.

We couldn't afford to go on a honeymoon because we put a lot of money into the wedding. We stayed at a hotel for the weekend. The night was going great. We were enjoying each other; however, I kept thinking about him being late for the wedding for some reason. So, I decided to ask him. I asked him why he was late. He said he was scared, and he thought I deserved better than him. I told him that I felt the same way. I told him that I thought it was normal to feel that way because it was happening. This weekend was fantastic. We had some time alone without the reality at home.

CHAPTER 10

THE HONEYMOON IS OVER

The honeymoon was over, and now it seemed like our life began to change. Months later, our second child was coming. One day after my husband arrived home from work, I was in so much pain that he had to rush me to the hospital as he entered the door. When we arrived at the hospital, our baby was coming. The nurses immediately started to prepare me for my delivery. Our baby was coming so fast, and the pain was unbearable. It was worse than my 1st pregnancy. When our baby arrived, it was a girl. We were shocked because the doctor told us she was a boy. When the nurse put her in my arms, I was in love again. She was 5 pounds 9 ounces, a beautiful baby girl.

Now I was blessed with 2 beautiful daughters. She came home the next day. We couldn't believe that she didn't cry that much. She was a happy baby. She smiled all the time. My husband was thrilled. I was so excited I dressed my girls like twins and did their hair alike. There is nothing like experiencing the joy of being a mom. Just thinking about them brings a smile to my face.

CHAPTER 11

DEJAVU

As the years went by, my husband's behavior started to change. I didn't understand what was going on. He started hanging out with one of his friends all the time. His friend's wife and I began to hang out, so the kids had play dates together, and we talked on the phone. We both were going through the same thing, so she knew what I was going through. Sometimes my husband wouldn't come straight from work. He would stay out in the morning hours. I talked about how I felt, and he threw me off and said he needed some space. He had to work, be a husband, and be a dad. I couldn't believe the man I was married to did not consider my feelings.

He told me I didn't have anything to worry about because he gave us everything we wanted and needed, and we did not lack anything. He did not realize that having money was not the only way to show love. He was a great provider, but he was not here physically and emotionally. I began to feel lonely and rejected. I felt that I was in this marriage alone. My daughters did not see their dad until mostly the weekends because they would be asleep when he got home.

I didn't know that in a marriage if a husband didn't want to come home at night to his family, he didn't have to base his feelings on it. If he feels like coming home, he would; if he didn't, he wouldn't. What kind of marriage is

If Only The Walls Could Hear

this? What happened to us becoming one? Wow! I can't get time off when I feel like it. If I wanted some time to myself, I had to get someone to watch the girls, but he didn't have any worries. This continued, so I took the girls, and we went to my parent's house. I gave him the space he needed. He started calling and coming down to my parents. After a week, I forgave him and returned home, and he started to stay home a little more.

After a year, my husband expressed a desire to purchase a house for us so the children could have a backyard to play in. He and I began to look for a house. We were excited we found our 1st house. Things were looking better. We started to go on dates 1 day a week and took the girls somewhere on Sundays. It started to feel like we were a family again. His dad was happy as well. Oh yes, his dad was still hanging in with us.

My husband began to hang out again as time went on with his friend. I talked to him again, and he started to be verbally abusive. I would try to hide it because I didn't want the kids and his dad to know. I started to go to church and prayed a lot more than ever. I used to seek counseling from the pastor. I prayed this marriage would get better. Looking from the outside, you wouldn't have known what was going on. It looked like the perfect marriage. He always showered me with good gifts and bought me a new car. I didn't know how to tell my parents what was going on. Every time I go, or we go as a family around my family and friends, I have to put on a happy wife mask-like everything is good.

He thought of showering me with gifts and making sure I always had money in my pocket for our girls and me. That should be enough. I was dying inside more and more every day. I remember asking God, why me? Was I being punished? When I saw what my mom was going through with my dad, did I speak this on myself? The only thing that kept me together was my daughters. They weren't asked to be in this situation. If only the walls could hear, I needed to talk to someone about the pain I was feeling. I had no one to talk to as the tears rolled down my brown cheeks. I wondered what I did to deserve this.

Teresa Sewell

Things got worse. His dad started to do things around the house that made it harder for me. I would clean the glass table in our living room. He would put his feet on it with his shoes on. I spoke with my husband about it. He would get upset and tell me to stop complaining, clean it up, and leave his dad alone. I was so crushed. I felt like a brick fell on my chest. I got outraged because it seemed like his dad had come before me. I was hurting so bad, and I had no one to talk to but the shame I was carrying. I don't know who I could tell. I balled up in a fetal position and held myself, and cried.

I stopped talking to him about things that bothered me. I didn't know what to do. I thought of leaving and letting him and his dad have the house together. I was too embarrassed to talk to anyone about it, what people would say and how I would take care of my daughters. I didn't want to change their lifestyle financially, nor did I want to take them out of the household with their dad. So I put up with whatever he did for their sake.

CHAPTER 12

FINDING MYSELF

I stayed, and I started a daycare in our home. This gave me something to do every day. I felt like I was doing something for myself. It also gave me some fulfillment. I was able to work while taking care of my kids. The 1st kid that I started caring for was my previous neighbor. She had 3 children. My kids were excited that they had someone to play with every day. I started to get more kids coming to the daycare. I asked my sister to move in to help me at the daycare. She agreed. She was a lot of help. I took the kids on field trips and taught them. The parents were very pleased with my services. They began to refer to others. It started to grow to become a real business. My husband was very supportive. He bought me a 15-passenger van so I could continue to take the kids on field trips. My girls were having a blast, and I was feeling accomplished.

My husband said it was time to get another house. We need more space now we have his dad, my sister, the girls they are getting older, the daycare, and him and I. So, house hunting we went.

We moved again, and we had more room. Our oldest is now 7, and the youngest is 6. I changed their schools again because they were not being challenged. I signed them up for different activities. My husband's cousin started a cheerleading squad at the park. My older daughter had to go to another squad when she was 9. My girls were getting to meet more kids. They are becoming more balanced now.

I introduced my sister to my oldest daughter's cheerleader coach. She began to hang out with my sister and me. The cheerleader coach would tell us everything was going on when she hung out with my sister and me.

My husband started to act strange again. He started to accuse me of cheating. I was wondering where that came from. He was starting back hanging out, and my sister and the girls started to ask why he wasn't coming home after work. I was embarrassed because now someone could see that our inside world was exposed and the perfect marriage didn't exist. She asked me if he was cheating, and I told her I didn't know. This went on for two years. My sister was in disbelief.

One Sunday, he and I were on the way to church. The kids stayed home with my sister. My husband told me that he has been cheating with my daughter's cheerleader coach for 2 years. I felt destroyed inside. I was crushed. I couldn't believe what I was hearing. I always had this feeling he wasn't faithful. I had dreams about him, and another woman and a baby, and I asked him if he got a woman pregnant. I took this as a sign from God. He would always tell me that I was crazy. He told me to stop accusing him of cheating because of dreams and my intuition. So now I know why my husband knew what was going on when I went out and why he had the phone tapped. The cheerleader coach would tell me everything was going on when she hung out with my sister and me. So, we arrived at the church, and the parking lot security officer asked my husband to pull over because there was a dead bird in the car front grill. The parking security officer got the bird out of the grill, and I told my husband to take me home because I could not control my tears. When we got home, I asked him to call her and let me talk to her, and he did. She confirmed everything that he said. He told her that he would work on his marriage, and she needed to work on her marriage. He wanted to keep his family. I left the house, and I called the one person that I would have never called, a person that told all my business to others. She met me, and we talked about it. I wasn't even thinking about her mouth running like water. My heart was torn, and I just needed to get away. She talked and calmed me down. I thanked her and left. I went riding to think about what I wanted to do next.

I began to think about all the late nights and coming home taking showers before he kissed me on my forehead. One morning, when he went to the car to work, his tires were flat. They had been slashed.

I asked him if he made someone mad, and he said that the cheerleader was the one that did it. He told her he wanted to end the relationship, and she was furious. There were so many signs that I chose to ignore. When I entered the house, I went home, and he came toward me crying, promising me he wouldn't hurt me anymore. I told him that I didn't want to talk to him to leave me alone. I prayed day after day, and I talked and prayed with my cousin, who was a pastor. She encouraged me not to give up on my marriage and let God handle this situation. So, I decided to forgive him.

CHAPTER 13

YES AGAIN

He asked if we could start over and renew our vows. I wanted to say no, but my mouth said yes. This is now our 10th year of marriage. So after renewing our vows

I still had to face her when I took the girls to practice. It was hard; however, my kids' happiness was the only thing that mattered. The coach found out that my husband and I had just renewed our vows, and she was angry. She started telling people at the park that she was pregnant by my husband, but she lost the baby. It made it hard to forgive my husband. I asked him about the baby, and he told me that she didn't tell him about the baby. He said it could have been by her husband. I asked him if this was ever going to end? He said yes. I chose to forgive, so I can't keep bringing it up. I had to be truthful with myself because every time he leaves the house, goes out with his friend, or comes home late, I think about it. I know he has to work on rebuilding the trust we had. I feel it will never be what it was. His father died months later after he told me about the affair, and I saw the cheerleader coach at the store, and she was in a wheelchair. She said she had a stroke. I didn't feel bad. Which was probably wrong. To be honest, I was thinking. It was payback from God because she knew he and I were married, and that was her Karma.

He started a new business, and we were making more money. Since we decided to start a new beginning, he wants to buy me a new house. House hunting, we went again. We kept all the houses we lived in and made their rental properties. So, I found the house this time alone. He told me to find what I wanted, and he would get it. The girls and I went to look for a house. We found a house; it was the one.

It had two levels, 2 and a half bathrooms, 3 bedrooms upstairs, an In-law suite downstairs, 2 kitchens, screen in porch, separate dining room, living room, family room with fireplace, and swimming pool. It was sitting on 1 acre of land with a driveway in the carport. I took him there with the realtor, and he loved it. We bought the house, and my family was amazed at the house. We had the kids' swim parties and plenty of barbecues he cooked. He could barbecue very well. He was so happy he stayed in the yard planting and strategizing about what he could put on the land. I felt like we were living a great life. The girls were on cloud nine. My sister moved out, and my other sister and daughter moved in. I set up the daycare in the in-law suite. It was a whole house downstairs, and the parents could bring the kids in the door down in the back of the house. We set up a playground and a basketball court on the other side of the house. The house was a fun, comfortable, and peaceful place.

Things seemed to be too perfect. I was scared something was going to happen. We met this couple of years later when the cheerleader coach was no longer at the park. My husband started to attend the girl's games they cheered for. While at one of the games, we met a couple was sitting by us at the game. We started hanging out with the couple. It was fun! The girls were older, so they stayed at home with my sister. She didn't have to watch them because they were at the age to take care of themselves. We started taking family vacations with them and their family and couple vacations together. I felt maybe he has grown out of that hanging-out stage. He started to do more family things. I started to have some feelings for him again. I started to trust him more.

Years went by, and we were enjoying life and family.

One night he told me that he needed to start going and advertise for the business, so he needed to go out to meet some people. He stayed out one night and didn't come until 6:30 in the morning. I thought something had happened to him. I asked why he stayed out. Immediately I started to think he was with a woman. At our shop, he had built a second floor at this point. So, he told me that he had been drinking and didn't want to risk driving that far home. I was heated! So, of course, I asked him if he was with a woman. He got upset, and he told me that he was grown and didn't have to explain anything to me. He was so loud he woke up everyone. I ask him to calm down. He was waking everyone up; of course, he didn't care. By this time, the girls were in high school, and they understood what was going on. He started to abuse the kids and me verbally. His bad temper was worse than ever.

One morning I woke up very sick. I found out that I had the flu. I passed out, and my husband stayed home from work to take care of me. The Sheriff came to our house to arrest my husband. I found out that a young lady had him arrested, saying he was stalking her and slashed her tires while taking care of me. So, he had a trial and was sentenced to 30 days in jail. My parents and sisters came to support him and me. We found out that he had an affair with her during the trial, and she wanted to end it, but he lost it. So, the girls started to ask where their dad was. I was so hurt and embarrassed to tell them their dad was in jail. I couldn't lie to them. The girls were starting to lose respect for him. They couldn't believe their dad was that kind of person. I was afraid because they knew he was on medication and didn't have any. I was so angry at him and myself because I couldn't forgive myself for accepting this behavior from him again. My parents now know that this perfect house is not perfect. I was embarrassed and relieved at the same time because I didn't have to play a role anymore and be truthful now. He got out of jail, and the cheating continued behind my back. One of our tenants said that my husband was trying to get with her, and she was married. She said she didn't know how to tell me because

I was such a sweet lady and didn't deserve him. She said he started to pop up at her house when her husband was at work, and she told him she wasn't interested. She was married and didn't pop up at the house; he still tried to convince her to be with him.

AS time went by, I would see condoms in my car. I asked why there were condoms in my car, and he tried to accuse me of having them. I continued to pray to God to get me out of this marriage. Plenty of nights, he would come home late and touch me and accuse me of cheating. I knew then he was having an affair. So, at night, I just lay there and cried because I needed to leave and didn't have the courage and the love for myself not to tolerate this behavior anymore. My girls, who were 15 and 16, began to lose respect for me. They ask me why I'm still with their dad. I was supposed to set an example for them to show them how a woman is supposed to be treated. You know how that made me feel. I believed I was doing the right thing by keeping them in the household with their father, even though this was not providing them with a healthy foundation as young girls.

CHAPTER 14

THE REJECTION

Now my husband was starting to get more verbally and physically abusive. Every time things didn't go his way, he got outraged. It got to the point that when he came home, the girls would go into their room and shut the door. He noticed that the girl's doors would be shut when he came home. He asked the girls to come into our room. He asks them why they permanently close their door when he gets home. Before they could answer, he told them not to have their door closed anymore when he got home because this was his house and they didn't pay any bills. I thought he was going to listen to his children's feelings. Boy, I was wrong. Then he started at me for allowing them to close their door. I told him I wasn't in the mood for that; I said if you didn't come home all the time with an attitude, we would welcome you home. He felt rejected.

He told me that I was turning the kids against him. He started calling them my kids. I was speechless. I couldn't believe he had got to that point to feel rejected that you would say something like that.

He was so angry he said to me that any woman would love to be in your position. You have this big house; you get anything you want, you're not lacking anything, and he never lets me forget it. He said you have a husband who ensures you all are provided for. He said that I had wasted so many years of his life and that he should go with his son. What? Say that again, you heard me right, my son. I was thrown off about what he said. I couldn't believe what I was hearing. What I thought I heard him say. I asked him what he meant by his son, and he said that he has this little boy that he mentored and called him his son. Oh, I felt like he realized what he let slip out, and now he is trying to change it. I ask why haven't I met him or heard you mention before now? He said that there wasn't any reason to mention him; he was just his mentor. My mind started drifting back into the past when I had those dreams about him holding a little boy. He always told me no. He was always saying stupid things that didn't make sense. He said I ought not to come back home. I don't want to come home arguing all the time. What did he mean? He was the one starting the arguments. I walked off, got in the shower, and started praying. I asked God to please get me out of this marriage without anybody getting hurt. I was over it. I started to look at him differently. It was as if my eyes started to close. I didn't want him to touch me anymore, I wasn't attractive to him, and I didn't want to be his wife anymore. I decided that it was time for a change.

CHAPTER 15

A NEW CHANGE

I prayed to God to show me the next step in my life. He put in my Spirit to go to hair school. I searched for cosmetology schools, found one, and enrolled. I told my husband and asked when I was going to start? I told him that I enrolled in the night classes. He was okay with it. I started school, and I felt like starting a new adventure. I was so excited, and now my girls could see their mom starting a new direction in her life, and they could be proud of and be an excellent example to them. This is something I started when my girls were 1 and 2 years of age, and I dropped out. After all, I couldn't concentrate because my girls were so young and were at home with their dad and grandfather. This was why this was so special because it was never too late. My girls were in high school, so I had the freedom to go back to finish what I had started. I was so focused on doing so well so I could make a life for my girls and me if their dad and I separated. I made an honor roll every semester until I graduated. I enjoyed going to school to get some self-time to reflect on my life. I can accomplish anything that I put my mind to. Sometimes, my husband would bring me food for dinner, making me feel like he supported my vision and dreams. That made me feel great inside.

Now it was time to graduate. I graduated with honors. I was so proud of myself. My husband took my family out after graduation. He was so supportive of me. After graduating, I told him that I wanted to turn the back room off the daycare and a hair salon. I wanted to fix the kids' hair. I found some salon equipment on Craigslist. I called the owner of the salon equipment and got some more information about the items. I spoke to my husband about it, and he said to go for it. I called the owner of the Salon equipment, and we agreed on a day for my husband and me to meet to see the equipment and possibly buy it. My husband and I met the seller, and we liked the equipment, paid for it, and went home. We set up the salon, and I was excited to start.

I told all the Childcare parents that I was starting a kid's salon in the back room of the childcare center. The parents were so excited for me. They started supporting my business. The parents made appointments for me to fix their children's hair while at work. My sister sat with the kids at naptime while I fixed the children in the daycare that had hair appointments. This was a brilliant Idea. I know now why God put it in my Spirit to start cosmetology school. I made so much money combining the childcare center with the salon. The childcare center started to grow even more significantly. I have a waiting list now. The parents were referring others to the daycare and the salon.

The business was doing Amazingly well. This was beginning to be a problem in the household and the marriage. My husband started acting weird again because I was making a lot of money. He started saying I didn't need him anymore. I told him that this was a good thing. There is no competition; this money is coming to the household. He told me that I was going to start acting differently. I ask myself if he is afraid of losing control.

CHAPTER 16

WHAT HAPPENED TO DADDY'S LITTLE GIRLS?

My husband used to make the most money. So, things started to get worse again. He would verbally abuse again. I ask him, why are you so angry all the time? In my mind, I was already planning my exit plan. By the way, I didn't mention that we had 2 dogs, a labradoodle, and an Australian poodle. My daughters loved their dogs. One day our dog got out of the door when someone came in. A woman was walking down the street holding a stick. Our labradoodle went up to her, and she said our dog bit her, but when I offered to clean her leg, she agreed. It looks like it came from the nails that were in the stick. She called the pound, and the pound came out to pick up our lab, but my husband was so mad that he had already taken her and given her away. The Sheriff asked where our dog was, so I called him at work. He started going off asking me why I answered the door. So, the Sheriff gave me a ticket to come to court because my husband took her away before the vet could test her for rabies and didn't tell the Sheriff where she was. He drove into the garage. My oldest daughter was crying because he took her dog away, and she loves her dogs. He came in and heard her crying, so he went into her bedroom and asked her to be quiet, and she asked him why he took her dog away and told her to be quiet. He was so cold. He was numb to our feelings. It crushed my oldest daughter because he wouldn't tell what he did with her dogs. My youngest daughter asked her dad if he could please tell her what he did with her sister's dog. He hit her, and she was trying to fight him back. She got away and went to call the police. He left the house and called me, asking did she call the police. I told him I didn't know. He came back home later, and he put her out of the house and told her not to come back. He said she was very disrespectful. I told him that he needs to start accepting that he needs some help to deal with his anger. What did I say that, for he went off saying he doesn't need help? He told me that I better not have my daughter in his house. I made arrangements for my daughter to live with a friend. I agreed with my friend that I would pay her to let my daughter live with her for a short time. He found out that I was paying my friend, and he told me that I better not give my friend anymore for our daughter. I continued to give her money. He asked me to start putting my money on the dresser when I got paid, and I told him No.

I said, I'm a mom, and I am not neglecting my daughter because of your anger. He got so mad and picked the remote control and threw it at me. He hit the wall and put a hole in it. Because I wasn't entertaining his behavior, he came to my side of the bed and started to pull my hair. I fell on the bed onto the floor, and he told me that if I tried to leave, nobody else wasn't going to have me. I felt like he must have blackout because of the rage and threats he was making. He was so angry. I called my oldest in the room and asked her to call the police, and I tried to take the phone out of my hand. He told her she better not call the police. I began to pray as he was pulling my hair, and God intervened, and he let me go. He went to pack some clothes and said he would move out. I never saw him cry like that. He finally left the house, and that is when we separated.

My husband cried and cried, and he said that the people he trusted, loved, and took care of financially betrayed him. He would have left a long time ago if he knew that would happen. I responded to him and said that financially isn't the only way to show love. He said I was ungrateful, and he left.

Teresa Sewell

Now that my husband has left the house, my oldest daughter and I are now enjoying peace and quietness. It feels great not to have any harmful or toxic energy in our home. I started to focus on my business and enjoy myself. I'm getting to know myself for a change. I cut my hair, got a new car, upgraded my business, started Barbering school, started dressing differently, and focused on getting closer to God. I felt like life was going in the right direction now. I felt like a new woman. I can think straight now; I'm starting to put my priorities back in order. I'm starting to hear the direction that God has for me. I feel so refreshed and renewed.

CHAPTER 17

NO MEANS NO.

Things were going well, and guess who started to show back up. My husband. He started just to pop up when he got ready. He must have forgotten that he doesn't live here anymore. He acts like everything is just average. He still thinks that I suppose to have sex with him and be his wife even though he left. He would show up at night while I was sleeping and just get in the bed and touch me. One night he came, and I was asleep, and he climbed in the bed and started to touch me, I asked him to please stop touching me, and he refused. I told him," No, leave me alone." I asked him to stop over and over again, he grabbed my arms and forced himself inside me.

I said to him, you are rapping me, and he responded with anger, rage and said, you are my wife; this is my body, and I can't rape what is mine; you are my wife. As I tried to move, I felt him putting more pressure on my body. All I could do was lay there in tears as he handled his business. I felt helpless. I couldn't believe that the man I was married to could do this to me. He has done many things, but not this took the cake. He treated me like a prostitute. As I looked into his eyes, he wasn't there. It was a look I had never seen before with him. After he finished, he rolled over off me as if nothing had just happened. I lay there in numbness, disbelief, and anger at what had just happened. I was angry at him and myself. I was angry because

God told me not to sleep with him anymore because he was sleeping with other women, but I couldn't stop him. Lord, please forgive me.

The following day when I woke up, my husband was gone. I lay in bed all day crying. My oldest daughter came into my bedroom to say good morning. I didn't want her to see me crying, so I rolled over on my stomach while talking to her. She asked me why did I turn over? My chest felt heavy, like bricks were on it. I couldn't let her see my face. I felt ashamed and nasty. How could I tell my daughter that her dad raped me last night? She sensed that something was wrong. I told her that I was tired and needed to sleep some more. She left my room, and I continued to cry.

CHAPTER 18

THE BLAME GAME

The week after the rape took place, my navel started to burn inside me; the feeling was unbearable. My oldest daughter took me to the emergency room. Her dad called my phone, and she told him that I was in the emergency room. He came to the hospital where I was. The doctor finally took me back to examine me. My husband showed up, and he stayed in the waiting room with my daughter. The doctor examined and took some lab work. The lab work showed that I had a sexual disease called Trich. I was devastated. I went to the waiting area angry, and he and my daughter asked me what the doctor said. I told him I had Trich. My daughter said it comes from meat. I responded that it is a sexually transmitted disease. My daughter and I left, and I went home. He pulled in the driveway shortly after we pulled in. I got in the bed, and he climbed in as well. I asked him, why are you getting in the bed with me?" He immediately started to get angry.

I asked him why he gave me a disease, and he accused me of sleeping with someone else, and they gave it to me. I was furious; I asked him not to put his arm around me. He got up and left.

Thus, two months later, I began to feel ill. . As the days went on, I was still feeling sick. I passed out while I was with a client. I went to the hospital, and they couldn't find anything wrong with me. I went home, and I started to feel sleepy all the time. My mouth was tasting metallic, so I began to eat a lot of pickles and ice cream with fries. At this time, I was attending barbering school, and it was hard. Sometimes I couldn't attend to my customers, and some of the students had to take over for me. I felt like I was going to pass out. One day my menstrual didn't show up. I found out I was pregnant for the 3rd time. I was so sick sometimes I couldn't attend school. I finally told my husband that I had just found out that I was 2months pregnant. He asked me if I was okay. I informed him that I had mixed feelings because I needed to work. I could not afford to be back on bed rest. He said I would take care of you. He came over to check on me and bought me a lot of mints for the taste in my mouth. Finally, I was able to go back to school. I felt fine until 2 days after returning to school. My back was hurting badly.

One of my classmates, whose station was next to mine, helped me go to the bathroom because I could hardly walk. As he shut the door and I began to pull down my pants and position over the toilet, the baby fell out in the toilet. I didn't know what to do. I just had a miscarriage; the instructor called my daughter and told her that I needed to go to the hospital. She took me there after I cleaned up, and they confirmed a miscarriage. I was so hurt. I had never lost a baby before. I told him the news, and he asked me if I wanted him to give me another baby. Wow, no kind of remorse. I was so hurt and devastated by my loss, and he did not understand that. I quickly told him NO and hung up the phone. I was grieving for a while. If the walls could only hear. I needed and wanted someone to hear me share my heart and pain and grief. Somebody I could tell how I was feeling in my mind, body, and emotions.

I was deeply hurt. I reached out to the one that did it to me, my husband. I ask him to come over to hold me. He came and held me all night. I felt vulnerable. I didn't care what he did to me at that time. I just needed someone to be there.

As time went on, he continued to come over more often to be with me. I was starting to let all my guards down with him.

CHAPTER 19

OH, HONEY, I AM DONE!!!

One night he told me he was coming over. Instead, he called me and said he needed to help his friend move. I said, okay. A few minutes later, my phone rang. His phone called me back, and he wasn't aware of it. I overheard him talking to a woman. I know it was God just bringing things to the light again. I stayed on the phone, and he continued to talk to the woman. As he talks, he is in a building with a high ceiling. Hearing their conversation continuing, I realized he was at the shop where he lived. So, I decided to go over to the shop and let him know that his phone had called me. My oldest daughter asked me where I was going, and she jumped in the car. We arrived at the shop. I knocked on the door, and he answered. He was shocked that it was me. He asked me what I was doing there and said I told you not to ever pop up at the shop. I didn't know what he was talking about. It did matter anyway. I just wanted him to know that I knew he wasn't moving furniture. I asked him if I could come in, and he told me I didn't need to. I told him I knew he had a woman there because his phone dialed me back. He looked dumbfounded. I tried to open the door, and he pushed me back to the point I was about to fall 20 or more stairs. I couldn't believe he was about to push me down the stairs. I asked him not to call or come around me again. I went down the stairs and got in my car. I was angry because my daughter had to see this. We saw him sitting down on the steps holding his head as we pulled off. My daughter and I just laughed on the way home. He started to call my phone all night. I finally answered, and he told me that he does massages now and the money was for me. I asked him when he went to school to do massages, and he said he learned on YouTube. I told him to leave me alone and never come around me again.

So, I prayed to God about my divorce, and they gave me the clearance to do so. I asked for confirmation, and it was confirmed. I asked God to send me an attorney he wanted me to have. Immediately God spoke to me and told me to call my cousin. I called my cousin and explained what was going on. He gave me the number of this couple that had their practice. He called them. They became my attorneys, and I began to pray and ask God about my divorce, and He confirmed for me to do so, so I filed for divorce.

He came over one day after I asked him not to anymore. He couldn't get in, so he called the police on me. My attorney called the police to let them know what was going on. The police came and let him in. He started telling the police that he lived there. I told the police he had left and moved into his shop and did not have anything here. The cop told him he wasn't supposed to leave his family to move to his shop instead of working with his family. He reasoned that he wasn't good enough. He said he moved there because he couldn't afford an alarm system.

I then told the police that I had just filed for a divorce. My husband exploded because he didn't know yet. After all, the holidays and the Sheriff's Dept. were slow. The police told me to give him a key. I was upset. He said it was still his house. I told the police I didn't have another key. The police told me that I needed to come up with one. The police left. He stayed. He told me he wanted his key now or wasn't leaving. I told him that I had to get one made. My husband started just getting out of hand. He threatened to take the door off the hinges. My oldest daughter, who lived with me, was there, and she started screaming and saying, dad, please stop. He went to his truck to get some tools to take the door off. She ran to her room and got her key and gave it to him so he would leave. He took the key and pulled off in anger. He called the phone minutes later and told me I better not have anyone in his house. He said If I can't have you, no one will. I hung up and called my attorney, and we went to file a restraining order so he could not come around me, and the judge denied it. The judge said I had to prove that he was a threat to me.

His divorce papers finally arrived, and he called me, and I didn't answer because I knew he had received them. He came to the house days after he got them and tried to change my mind.

He said he would never marry anyone else. I will always be his wife. He tried to get me to sleep with him, and I told him no. I am no longer interested in you. I don't see you in that way anymore.

He finally called me 2 weeks later to discuss the properties we owned and the shop. I told him that we had to discuss it through our attorneys. He got angry and said, we don't need an attorney. We can handle this ourselves. I disagreed. I didn't trust him because I knew he could be controlling. So, I told him no. I got off the phone. I called my attorney to let him know that he had called me. My attorney told me to let him handle it and not talk to him about what he is for.

I started to feel stressed out because I didn't want to fight over material things. I went on a fast for a couple of days, and I heard the Lord tell me to give everything except the house I was living in. God also told me to call one of my lady cousins. She ends up calling me after I stop praying. I told her that I was just about to call her because I needed to have a discussion with her about my marital assets. She began to tell me that she left home with nothing just to have peace in her life and mind. I knew then that was my answer. I felt peace immediately about the discussion I needed to make. I called my soon-to-be ex-husband and told him he could have everything but the house we were living in and the car I was driving, and he had to fix the septic tank in the yard and the holes he put in the walls. I didn't want anyone to think that I wasn't trying to split things with you. I responded that it was between you and myself. I didn't want my daughters to have to see

Teresa Sewell

their parents fighting over material things. So, he finally agreed with me. I called my attorney, and he wrote up the papers for me to sign. Now it's time for divorce day, and his attorney rescheduled it. This went on several times until the judge finally said he would give me the divorce. We were not going to wait any longer. Yes, I'm divorced now. I felt like a kid in a candy store and a prisoner getting out of jail. I'M FREE!!!!

I could not go through this journey without the word of GOD. Below is some scripture that helped me. I pray that these words strengthen you to continue to believe and trust God as you move forward.

~REJECTION~

John 1:11 NLT

He came to his people, and even they rejected him.

Psalm 27:10 ASV

10 When my Father and mother forsake me, Then Jehovah will take me up.

~ BROKEN HEARTED~

Psalm 147:3

He heals the brokenhearted and binds up their wounds.

Psalm 34:17-18

The righteous cry out, and the Lord hears them; He delivers them from all their troubles. The Lord is close to the brokenhearted and saves those who are crushed in Spirit.

~FAMILY ~

Colossians 3:19 NIV.

Husbands, love your wives, and do not be harsh with them.

Colossians 3:13 NIV

Bear with each other and forgive one another if any of you has a grievance against someone. Forgive as the Lord forgave you.

MARRIAGE, ~

Matthew 19:4-6 NIV

"Haven't you read," he replied, "that at the beginning the Creator 'made them male and female,' and said, 'For this reason, a man will leave his father and mother and be united to his wife, and the two will become one flesh? So they are no longer two, but one flesh. Therefore, what God has joined together, let no one separate."

Hebrews 13:4 NIV

Marriage should be honored by all, and the marriage bed kept pure, for God will judge the adulterer and all the sexually immoral.

DARKNESS~

Psalm 23:4 NIV

Even though I walk through the darkest valley, I will fear no evil, for you are with me; your rod and your staff, they comfort me.

Isaiah 41:13 NIV

For I am the Lord your God who takes hold of your right hand and says to you, Do not fear; I will help you.

SELF LOVE~

1 John 4:18 NIV

There is no fear in love. But perfect love drives out fear because fear has to do with punishment. The one who fears is not made perfect in love.

Colossians 3:9-10 NIV

Do not lie to each other, since you have taken off your old self with its practices and have put on the new self, which is being renewed in knowledge in the image of its Creator.

GOD IS GOOD

1 Chronicles 16:34 NIV

Give thanks to the Lord, for he is good; his love endures forever.

Nahum 1:7 NIV

The Lord is good, a refuge in times of trouble. He cares for those who trust in him.

FAITH

Matthew 21:22 ESV

And whatever you ask in prayer, you will receive if you have faith.

Hebrews 11:6 ESV

And without faith it is impossible to please him, for whoever would draw near to God must believe that he exists and that he rewards those who seek him.

~TRUST~

Proverbs 3:5 Esv

Trust in the Lord with all your heart, and do not lean on your understanding.

Psalm 56:3-4 ESV

When I am afraid, I trust you. In God, whose word I praise, I trust; I shall not be frightened. What can flesh do to me?

INFIDELITY ~

Proverbs 6:32 ESV

He who commits adultery lacks sense; he who does it destroys himself.

Exodus 20:14

"You must not commit adultery."

MONEY

Hebrews 13:5 NIV

Keep your lives free from the love of money and be content with what you have because God has said, "Never will I leave you; never will I forsake you."

1 Timothy 6:10 NIV.

For the love of money is the root of all kinds of evil. Some people, eager for money, have wandered from the faith and pierced themselves with many griefs.

SELF CONTROL

Titus 2:11-12

For the grace of God has appeared that offers salvation to all people. It teaches us to say "No" to ungodliness and worldly passions and live self-controlled, upright, and godly lives in this present age...."

2 Timothy 1:7 (GNT)

For the Spirit that God has given us does not make us timid; instead, his Spirit fills us with power, love, and self-control

CHANGE

James 1:17 CEB

Every good gift, every perfect gift, comes from above. These gifts come down from the Father, the Creator of the heavenly lights, whose character is no change.

Numbers 23:19 CEB

God isn't a man that he would lie or a human being who would change his mind. Has he ever spoken and not done it, promised and not fulfilled it.

BIRTH

John 16:21 ESV

She is sorrowful when a woman gives birth because her hour has come. Still, when she has delivered the baby, she no longer remembers the anguish, for joy that a human being has been born into the world.

Luke 1:14 ESV

And you will have joy and gladness, and many will rejoice at his birth,

JEALOUSY

Mark 7:21-23 ESV

Out of man's heart, from within come evil thoughts, sexual immorality, theft, murder, adultery, coveting, wickedness, deceit, sensuality, envy, slander, pride, and foolishness. All these evil things come from within, and they defile a person.

Song of Solomon 8:6-7 ESV

Set me as a seal upon your heart, as a seal upon your arm, for love is strong as death, jealousy is fierce as the grave. Its flashes are flashes of fire, the very flame of the Lord. Many drinks of water cannot quench love, neither can floods drown it. If a man offered for love all the wealth of his house, he would be utterly despised.

FEELING INVISIBLE

Genesis 16:13 NIV

She gave this name to the Lord who spoke to her: "You are the God who sees me," for she said, "I have now seen[a] the One who sees me."

Luke 12:6-7 NIV

Are not five sparrows sold for two pennies? Yet not one of them is forgotten by God. 7 Indeed, the very hairs of your head are all numbered. Don't be afraid; you are worth more than many sparrows.

FACING THE TRUTH

And now it begins. I have to face the reality that I no longer have the man I called husband, Lover, daddy, provider, protector, and friend. I was so excited to be free from him, but I didn't realize that I was still holding myself in a jail cell without bars. My mind is running with the woulda, coulda, shoulda in my life.

How do I get free? NOW, what's next for me?

www.ingramcontent.com/pod-product-compliance
Lightning Source LLC
Chambersburg PA
CBHW051710090426
42736CB00013B/2633